Internet Marketing for Small Business

How to Develop an Effective Strategy for Your Business

By Carl Willis

Simplicity Marketing LLC

Internet Marketing for Small Business by Carl Willis
Published by Simplicity Marketing LLC; Wichita, KS

www.SimplicityMarketingLLC.com

For permissions contact:
info@SimplicityMarketingLLC.com

Table of Contents

Introduction

"If you build it, they will come..." Any movie buff knows this is the famous line from "Field of Dreams." While this thought may work well in a movie plot about building a baseball diamond in the middle of corn field in Iowa, it is not a great plan for an internet marketing strategy.

As a marketing consultant, I continually encounter business owners who bought into this philosophy. They built the website, set up the Facebook page, created a Twitter handle and yet their phone is not ringing, nor are their sales increasing. Simply having these online properties does not guarantee that anyone will visit them.

Over the next few chapters, I will be showing you how to develop a comprehensive marketing strategy that is both inescapable and irresistible to your most profitable prospect audience. Once deployed, you will chuckle every time a prospect says: "I see you everywhere...."

Carl Willis, Marketing Strategist
Simplicity Marketing LLC

Chapter 1 – Know Thy Audience

When it comes to marketing online, you must begin with the end in mind. The first and most important question is this: "Who is my most profitable customer?" Many business owners will quickly answer that everyone is their prospect. There is a group that is much more likely to do business with you, in greater quantities and with greater frequency. Getting clear on the makeup of this audience is critical, as it will guide every other aspect of your online marketing efforts.

If you are an existing business, your customer records will help you refine this ideal customer profile much quicker. If you are just starting out, you will need to do some leg work to create an accurate profile. In either case, here are some questions to help you begin to fine tune this profile:

- Is this individual male or female?
- How old are they?
- Are they married, divorced, single, widowed, etc...
- Do they have children?
  - How many?
  - What ages?
- Do they rent or own their own home?
  - How many years have they lived there?
- Are they pet owners?
- Are they active in a faith based community?

- What type of work does this individual do?
    - Full-time or part-time?
    - Satisfied with their career?
    - Blue collar or white collar?
- What type of hobbies does this individual have?
- What kind of car do they drive?
- What television shows do they watch?
- What types of books do they read?
    - Do they prefer eBooks or traditional books?
- What type of music do they listen to?
- What are their dreams?
- What are their concerns and sources of stress?

At first you might think this is overkill for profiling a customer, but let me show you the power of defining your ideal customer profile or "avatar" this way.

Here is an avatar that I use in one of my business lines. We'll call him Brad.

Brad is in his late 40's. He has been married for 22 years. He has been a mid-level corporate manager for the past 15 years, working for the same employer for the past 5. Brad has 3 children. One is grown and starting their own career, one is finishing college and the youngest one is in high school. Brad is part of the "sandwich generation" taking care of an aging parent, having already faced the death of the other parent. Brad is unsatisfied in his current job, but he stays for the health insurance. He would love to travel more, but his limited amount of vacation and the demands of family prevent him from doing so. Brad dreams of doing charitable work after he retires, but has no clear-cut plan for retirement. Brad loves 70's rock and 80's pop music. He drives a late model pickup or sedan and his wife drives an SUV. Brad is an avid sports fan who actively plays fantasy football and watches his favorite team on television anytime he gets the chance.

By taking the time develop the avatar of Brad, it is much easier to develop the appropriate marketing strategy to communicate our message in such a way that it resonates with him and his current place in life. The result that drives everything else is the need to connect with Brad on an emotional level, causing him to resonate with the message being presented.

In decades past, we could simply bombard Brad with a marketing message through traditional forms of advertising such as radio, newspaper and television; however, in today's digital world those mediums may never reach him. We now live in an age of attraction marketing, where we must draw our target audience to us through the content and engagement we create online.

The greatest mechanism for drawing out your avatar is expertise. Position yourself as the recognized expert and authority in your field and those you are trying to connect with will seek you out in their quest for information. It is from this position of expertise that we will develop your "marketing eco-system."

Chapter 2 – Marketing Eco-System

In creating a marketing eco-system, you are creating a virtual spider web for your product brand or service. Think of this analogy, a moth flies into a spider's web. The moth discovers that its nose is now stuck to the web, so it begins to flap its wings. The left wing sticks to the web, then the right. The moth begins to move its legs and they also stick to the web. Before long, the moth is fully attached to the spider web and it is not going anywhere else.

It is generally accepted that a prospect needs a minimum of seven exposures on average to a marketing message prior to making a buying decision. One of the common mistakes that so many business owners make is the lack of follow up exposures to the initial exposure. This why so many business websites generate little to no sales activity, because the site is the one and only exposure the prospect ever gets to the marketing message.

By creating a marketing eco-system, we are ensuring that our prospect gets multiple exposures through multiple modes of online communication. Each exposure reinforces the message of the previous exposures, until a buying decision is made or the prospect is no longer a qualified buyer of your products and services.

In world of traditional marketing, we see this principle at work with the soft drink and beer companies. Their logo, image and name is literally everywhere:

- Delivery trucks
- Restaurant signs
- Sports venues
- Athletic apparel
- Grocery stores
- Billboards
- Television
- Radio
- Websites
- Cups
- Coolers

The brand becomes inescapable and immediately recognizable. Even if a person is not an end consumer of the product, they are very clear as to the message of the product or service.

In our eco-system, we will be using a similar principle with one key distinctive. Our marketing will be laser focused on our avatar. We want to maximize the efficiency of our communications, so they are only engaged by the most likely of prospective customers.

Chapter 3 – Your Website

Your website is the center of your marketing eco-system universe. This could also be a landing page, social media page or video channel; however, for most businesses this will be their website as it is the primary location for customer engagement, feedback and sales of your product or service.

With this understanding, it is imperative that your website be set up to effectively move your prospect from one level to the next of the buying cycle. Here are three components of engagement that need to be built into your site:

1. **Communicate** – your site should clearly communicate who you are, what you are about, the problem that you solve, the steps necessary to utilize your product or service, testimonials and reviews, a call to action.

2. **Capture** – your site should include a mechanism for collecting leads. At the very minimum, this should be an email address, but ideally a name and phone number are best. As a side note, the more information you request the fewer leads you will collect; however, the quality of the leads generated will be much higher.

3. **Connection** – Your site should have a means of connecting your prospects to additional points of

engagement in your eco-system. These could be addition to your mailing list, subscription to your site feed and connection to your social media channels. The more points of connection a prospect has with you, the more loyal they will become to your brand. Additionally, you create backup systems to your other modes of prospect communication.

When developing your website, it is important that each of these components be above the fold on the page. This means simply that these components are visible to your site visitor without having to scroll further down the page.

Your website should be optimized not only for textual communication, but also for visual communication through images and video. The trend in internet usage is towards mobile platforms, so imagery is just as important as the words that are printed on the page. It is often the images that keep your visitors engaged on the site for longer periods of time.

Do not lose sight of the main objective on your site, converting that visitor into a prospect and eventually a customer. Too many sites are built as a source of information, without ever calling the visitor to take an action. What is the ultimate action you want that visitor to take? Should they call you now, fill out the response form, schedule an appointment, request a quote or place a product in the shopping cart? Every aspect of the site should be designed with that result in mind.

Unfortunately, far too many websites are designed with form in mind and totally disregard function. A good web designer is a great asset, but don't depend on the designer to view the site with a marketer's eye. Build your sites with a clear purpose, not just a fuzzy ideal.

In the remaining chapters, we will break down the spokes of the eco-system and how to use each of these systems to demonstrate your expertise and drive highly targeted, highly engaged traffic into your site, for the purpose of transacting business.

Chapter 4 – Blogging for Business

In the early 2000's the online world was introduced to the concept of a blog. Blogs originally started as an online journal where individuals could record their thoughts, ideas and opinions for public consumption. It wasn't long before savvy entrepreneurs realized that a blog was a powerful mechanism for demonstrating leadership and expertise in a particular field or industry.

Blogs quickly became a favorite of the major search engines, as the content was considered fresh and relevant. This led to the creation of more robust and highly functional blog platforms such as WordPress, which is now the most commonly used platform for website creation.

Before we get into the how-to of blogging, let's look at the reasons why this needs to be a key part of your eco-system.

1. When structured correctly, each blog post becomes a mini-website on the topic of the post content.
2. Blog post content can be matched up to actual search queries.
3. Blog posts are designed for reader engagement through comments and sharing.

Ideally, you want to utilize a self-hosted WordPress blog as your blogging platform. In most cases, WordPress is the website platform being utilize, so this is a core functionality of the website design. A self-hosted blog will be hosted through a hosting company such as GoDaddy or Hostgator. This is important, so that you retain rights to the content on the site.

When structuring a blog post, begin by thinking about your avatar. What would that ideal prospect be searching for in their buying process? Some of the common search queries revolve around how to do something, user reviews, customer complaints and pricing research. Each of these concepts are an opportunity to capture the search and demonstrate your expertise on the subject matter.

For example, our avatar is thinking about buying a pickup truck. Here are some potential searches they might be performing:

- Buying new vs. used pickup truck
- Best reliability pickup truck
- User reviews pickup trucks
- Which pickup truck has the best warranty
- Financing a new pickup truck
- How to choose the best pickup truck

Each of these search queries could be the topic of a unique blog post. Ideally, you would use the search query as your title. The search query should be used in the first sentence and the last paragraph of the blog post as well. Break the content into subsections with variations of the search query or related terms as the subheadings. The post should be no less than 500 words and ideally should be between 1,000 and 2,000 words to sufficiently demonstrate expertise and cover the topic thoroughly. Include at least one image relating to the topic of the blog post and put a call to action at the end of your blog post.

When your blog posts answer the questions your prospect has you become a trusted advisor. As a trusted advisor, your recommendations carry more weight and bypass the resistance normally encountered in a typical sales presentation. For example, your doctor doesn't have to sell you on a prescription, simply informs and advises and prescribes. The more expertise you consistently demonstrate the more effective your sales process becomes.

Chapter 5 – Repurposing for More Content

Once a blog post is written a magical world of replication opens to you. Your blog posts can be repurposed as articles, reports, white papers, .pdf documents, podcasts, email broadcasts and more.

Let's begin with articles. One of the easiest forms of repurposing is to submit your blog post to article directories such as ezinearticles.com, niche specific ezines and other online journals pertaining to your industry. It should be noted that directories such as ezinearticles.com do require that your content be original, so you will want to do a re-write of your original blog post prior to submitting to these directories.

Reports and white papers are another great way to repurpose your blog content. These informational pieces can be a great source of lead generation when you ask a prospect to provide their email address so a download link can be sent to them. When this is done, the prospect now becomes an active subscriber to your email list. Keep your reports informational in nature and place a strong call to action at the end with a point of connection such as a website or phone number.

.pdf documents are often overlooked as a form of repurposing content. This is a big mistake. The search engines index .pdf documents, so this creates a great ranking opportunity for your content. Additionally, live links can be inserted into the .pdf document, allowing your reader to immediately click over to a website or offer that is being referenced in the document. You can easily convert your blog posts to .pdf format at printfriendly.com. Once the post is converted to .pdf upload the document to sites such as studysoup.com and slideshare.net.

Read your blog post and record it using open source recording software like Audacity. Once the recording is made convert the file to .mp3 format and upload to a podcast hosting site. These podcasts can then be distributed via iTunes and other audio distribution channels.

Blog posts make great email content for your customer and subscriber lists. Repurpose your blog posts as a single email or email series to further educate your audience and demonstrate your expertise once again. Any opportunity to reconnect with your audience will prove valuable.

In addition to the above repurposing ideas, you can also repurpose your blog content as video segments and article content for offline publications.

Chapter 6 – Video Marketing

We all know that video is a powerful medium for communicating a message. Apart from face to face interaction, video is one of the most effective mechanisms for developing trust between a vendor and a prospect.

Here are some additional reasons you should be using video as a component of your marketing eco-system. YouTube is the 2nd largest search engine in the world. Google owns YouTube and quickly indexes video uploads. A video will often outrank written content in search engine results.

As mentioned in the previous chapter, video is one of the ways that your blog content can be repurposed. To do this simply title the video with the same title as your blog post. In the video description list your website url and/or phone number in the first line, followed by the title of the video. Complete the description with one or two paragraphs from your blog post and place a call to action at the end. You will want to tag your video with the keywords from the blog post.

Videos should be no more than 2-3 minutes to maximize user engagement. If your content is longer, create a series of videos. Make sure that your background doesn't distract from the message of the video and make a call to action at the end.

With today's technology, you can quickly and easily record high quality video content using a smartphone or tablet. For those who are intimidated by the camera, you can do a screen capture recording of a PowerPoint presentation. In this type of video, you will simply speak the narration as you screen record your presentation.

You might also want to consider hiring a professional actor or spokesperson to record your content. Fivver.com is a great resource for finding these professionals. Most will charge a set amount per number of words being spoken on camera. This is a great option when a personal connection is important, but the business owner is not confident or simply does not come across well on camera.

If you are recording your own videos remember to look directly down the lens of the camera and speak directly to the camera. Looking away to read scripts or away from the camera can distract from the message and leave the viewer with a sense of mistrust towards your message. Make sure you get very comfortable with your subject matter before hitting record.

If you are going to use any type of background music or graphics, make sure you have usage rights for those items or use public domains content. Improperly used content is one of the primary reasons that YouTube channels get shut down.

At the end of each video you should create two calls to action. The first call to action is to become a subscriber of your channel. The second call to action is to take advantage of your offer, visit your website, call or engage on some other form of communication.

Make sure to brand your channel to your business. This includes the channel graphics, channel icon and channel description. Your website should be prominently displayed in the description.

In addition to YouTube there are also other video sharing sites that can be incorporated into your marketing strategy. These include sites like Vimeo, Viddler and Dailymotion.

Chapter 7 – Social Sharing

Social sharing or social bookmarking as it is also known, is a platform for syndicating your blog posts, articles, documents and videos to a wider audience. In theory, social sharing works this way. You find a piece of content that you find helpful, funny or informative and you bookmark it so others with the same interests can find it.

Most social sharing sites allow you to create categories or assign the bookmark to existing categories of interest. When sharing your content socially, it is important that your own content only be a portion of what you share. Social media is all about community, so you want share the content of others as well as your own. A good ratio for sharing is approximately 2/3 of your shares are the content of others and 1/3 is your own.

When you share content also be sure to leave some type of description or comment about the content you are sharing. This will help others evaluate your content with more receptivity, because you are engaging the audience.

Some of the top social sharing sites you should include are StumbleUpon, Digg, Delicious and Reddit. Not only do these sites have their own strong communities, but the links from these sites back to your site can create high authority, high value back links for search engine ranking purposes.

Chapter 8 – Forums

A forum is an online bulletin board where people assemble around a common interest. Forums are often used for advice, how to information, user reviews and recommendations.

To gain maximum benefit from a forum, be sure to completely fill out your user profile and include a link to your website in your profile description. When engaging with other users on the forum, provide valuable insights and information that demonstrate your expertise in the niche or interest that the community is built around.

Product sales pitches are generally frowned upon inside of the forum environment. This is where your written and video content become invaluable. As part of your answer to a question or line of discussion you can refer other readers to the content you have created on that topic at either your blog or your video channel. How to articles and videos work very well in this environment.

Chapter 9 – Social Networking

When most business owners talk about "social media" what they are really referring to is social networking. These would include the primary social networks: Facebook, LinkedIn, Google+ and Twitter. Social networks can be a place of syndication and bookmarking, but they are best used as a platform for audience engagement.

Remember our avatar, Brad, from earlier in the book. Finding Brad has never been easier than it is with the social networking sites. Simply begin to search for the demographics, employers, hobbies and interests of Brad and you can quickly find a nearly inexhaustible pool of prospects that match his profile.

First let me give a brief overview of each of the primary social networks so you better understand how to utilize them in your eco-system.

- Facebook – the dominate player in social networking. The site currently has over 1 billion users worldwide. Statistically over half of the active users on this network access their account at least once per day. Facebook provides individual user profiles, business pages and affinity groups. Individual users also have the ability to live broadcast on their timeline. This network also has a robust advertising platform that allows you target by behaviors and interests.

- LinkedIn – this network is the meeting place for business professionals. Some statistics estimate the annual income of the average user to be $120,000 per year.   LinkedIn provides both personal profiles and company pages.

- Google+ - this network was originally designed to compete with Facebook, but has since morphed into a central business hub for virtual meetings, Google maps listings and business pages. Individuals can also have an active profile on Google+ which is vital for authorship on blog posts and additional indexing opportunities in search engine results.

- Twitter – this network is a micro-blogging site. User tweets are limited to 140 characters. Many notable celebrities and politicians are active Twitter users. Twitter now offers image and video sharing as well as live broadcasts via Periscope.

Effective social networking is all about engagement with your audience. As your following grows you want to engage your audience with valuable topics and information. One of the first items that should be addressed on any social network is a complete profile. Create a timeline banner, profile picture and description for each profile. Include your website address in your profile description and invite people to like your page, connect with you as a friend or follower, connect with you on your other social media channels and even subscribe to your email list.

Social networking is becoming increasingly visual as more users access these networks through their mobile devices. Use images and videos for maximum exposure and higher levels of engagement with your audience.

When someone engages with our content, be sure to communicate with them. Thank them for liking, sharing or commenting. Respond to their comments and messages in a timely manner. Many businesses are finding that their audience is choosing to communicate almost exclusively through social media messages and private message functions.

Balance is critical in your social networking. Approximately 80% of your posting should be social, informative or entertaining in nature. The remaining 20% can be a direct offer or promotion. When these ratios are ignored, the audience will quickly tune out your message.

Look for affinity groups on the social network that you can join. As a member of these groups interact regularly with other group members. Like their posts, leave comments and share content. Demonstrate your expertise with helpful posts that are strictly content. A blog post or video can easily be repurposed as a post into these groups.

Social networking has the power to increase your "know, like and trust" factor rapidly and exponentially, since your audience can engage with you in real time. The more authentic and approachable you become in social media, the more comfortable your audience will be with progressing the relationship into a business relationship.

For Facebook you will want to establish a business page. This is done for two primary reasons. Facebook provides excellent analytical information on your audience, thus allowing you to develop your message and offers to reflect the character of the audience. The second reason is the Facebook Ads platform. This robust advertising platform allow you to engage large audiences at a very cost effective price, using Facebook's interest and behavioral data for laser focused targeting.

Your best results with a social network will come from keeping the engagement within the social network. Instead of referring another user to your website, refer them to your business page instead or to another piece of content in your social media profile.

Chapter 10 – Buy Your Traffic

Most methods described in this book are considered "free" or organic marketing methods, because they require no financial expenditure in and of themselves. Paid advertising on the other hand does require continual financial investment, but is also a very efficient way to bring large amounts of targeted traffic into your marketing eco-system.

Paid advertising can take on numerous forms. These could include pay-per-click advertising, banner advertisements, solo ads, cost-per-view advertising and contextual ads. For the sake of simplicity, we will focus on two primary strategies: Search pay-per-click and Facebook Ads.

- Search pay-per-click – these ads are displayed with search results on any of the major search engines. The two largest ad networks are Google AdWords and the Yahoo/Bing network. In this type of advertising, an advertiser bids for search terms based on a cost per click pricing structure. These ads are triggered when a search user searches for a keyword or phrase that matches the search term bids. The power of this type of advertising is the engagement during the active search process.

- Facebook Ads – these ads are displayed on the user's timeline, right sidebar, Instagram and Facebook ad network. Unlike search ads, Facebook ads are targeted based on demographic, behavioral and interest targeting. Ads can be used to increase engagement, direct to a website, increase conversions or grow an audience.

These two advertising strategies also incorporate retargeting or remarketing capabilities. This means that a visitor to your website can be tracked with a pixel. This allows the business owner to create a separate advertising audience made up exclusively of prior visitors to their website. A unique message and offer can be created uniquely for these individuals. Retargeting campaigns typically display the advertising across multiple websites and platforms.

When utilizing paid advertising, it is critical that you monitor your cost per acquisition and earnings per click. If these factors are not monitored, ineffective ads, poor targeting and other factors can exhaust your budget quickly.

Paid traffic is best used when there is a clearly defined sales process for leads created through your advertising or to enhance a promotional offer or event.

Chapter 11 – Email Marketing

"The money is in the list." This has been the mantra of internet marketers for years. Your email marketing list is the most valuable asset you have in our online marketing. Once a prospect has opted in to your email list, you can communicate with them over and over. The longer that prospect remains on your email list, the more offers they will be exposed to, thus creating the opportunity or repeat sales without the cost of acquiring a new customer.

To create a growing marketing list you will need an auto responder platform. Some of the most widely used auto responder platforms are AWeber, Get Response, Constant Contact and MailChimp. These platforms will give you the ability to create lead capture forms, automated follow up messages and scheduled broadcasts.

An email list is best grown using an offer In exchange for the contact information of the prospect. This offer could be regular coupons and specials, a special report, a white paper, a free webinar or video series that fills a need. When your prospect enters their information, they will be asked to confirm that request (double optin), verifying that you have been given permission to add them to the mailing list.

As with the social marketing strategies we covered, balance is critical in your email marketing. Approximately four out of every five marketing emails should be all content, delivering value to your audience and once again demonstrating your expertise. These emails can have a call to action in the P.S. section. The remaining emails can be a direct offer.

All of your emails should have an unsubscribe link that allows your prospect to opt out of any future emails. The email marketing platforms will automate this process for you to remain compliant with the CAN-SPAM act.

In addition to a prospect list, you will also want to build an email list of current and past customers. The messages sent to your customer list will be a continuation of the dialogue between customer and business owner. Alert your customers to new products, services and specials.

All of your online properties should direct your prospects to either your website or an alternative landing page where they can easily be added to your email subscriber list.

Conclusion

When you create a marketing eco-system and consistently provide value to your audience, your marketing becomes magnetic. Hot prospects will seek you out and look to do business with you and you alone, because you are the recognized expert and authority in your field.

If you would like to develop the marketing eco-system for your business, please contact our offices today for a complimentary consultation.

For additional marketing training, visit http://simplicitymarketingllc.com/internet-marketing-training-courses/

About the Author

Carl Willis is a serial entrepreneur who has been training and equipping leaders in multiple professional disciplines for over 20 years. He is a highly sought after speaker who speaks on a diversity of topics including social media marketing, Facebook marketing, online lead generation, leadership and personal development.

Through his company, Simplicity Marketing LLC, Carl developed the processes and systems that have allowed him to build multiple online business ventures. Utilizing these skills, Carl works closely with small business owners globally, helping them to apply the principles of attraction marketing to grow their online business presence and gain a marketplace advantage over the competition.

In addition to his business pursuits, Carl travels frequently to East Africa and India working with local church leaders and mission organizations to better serve their communities. This work is now providing tuition, food and health care for orphaned children who would otherwise live in the streets, as well as creating businesses to fund those initiatives on a local level.

Invite Carl to speak at your next event or meeting:

http://carlwillis.com/speaking/

Carl's Blog

carlwillis.com

Connect Further

Simplicity Marketing LLC
simplicitymarketingllc.com

Facebook
https://www.facebook.com/simplicitymarketingllc

Twitter
https://twitter.com/SimplicityMrktg

LinkedIn
https://www.linkedin.com/in/carlwillis

Google+
https://plus.google.com/+CarlWillis70

YouTube
https://youtube.com/homebizsimplicity

Made in the USA
San Bernardino, CA
05 June 2018